The Invention Tree

The Invention Tree

Jerome McGann

with pictures by
Susan Bee

chax press
2012

copyright © 2012 by Jerome McGann
images copyright © 2012 by Susan Bee
all rights reserved

ISBN 9780925904 09 6

Chax Press
411 N 7th Ave Ste 103
Tucson, Arizona 85705-8388
USA

For

Virgil Burnett

Il est caché parmi sur l'herbe

千万両

One

In a Land Transoceanic
Past the vast Immensett Sea,
By the river Twaddlequiver
Rose the great Invention Tree,
Guarded in a garden closely
By Lord Luminosity.
In serapes and sarongs,
There the Bos and Nims and Dongs
Grow up pictures, poems, and songs,
In the Land Transoceanic
Past the vast Immensett Sea.

Two

Ages ancient and anterior

Hid in beatific bowers,

Stirred a Vision Bird to tell of

Flagrant hands with dreamy powers

Flicking flakes of fragrant showers

Hours and hours on vagrant flowers.

"'T is our Being Beatific

(Sang the Bird in tones terrific)

Our amazing beatific

Lady Luminosity

Lady Luminosity."

Three

But on Isolation Island
Ruled the demons Don't and Never,
Among rocks and scrubby sages
Skinny characters and clever
Fixing number, weight, and measure,
To translate and name that treasure
With their strict insistency,
That creation of the Lady,
The Impossabilla Tree
Skinny demons Don't and Never
Dried-up demons Don't and Never!

Four

Lady blively, magic, sainted,

Scans her land majestically

"Would that once upon our Wood Land

Grew a great Invention Tree!"

Trochees straight turn anapaestics

Wood Lands dream of hypermetrics,

(Don't and Never turn dyspeptics —

"Rhymes and lines are running free!")

"Homonymphs and Synonymphies

Call the Dimplies and the Simplies

And the Smarties and the Pimplies

Para no masiacly

Para no messiacly."

Five

Then the little letters lightly
Litter light along those lawns,
While the long are lighting out for
Limpid glimpses of that dawning
Where the Funny Nims, reborn,
Watch the Silly Belles of morning,
Lyric ladies, ludic, lisping,
Unheard melodies are listing —
All the nymphs are unresisting
Where the long and little letters
Lightly lisp along the lawn.

Six

"What? a Would Land in a Wood Land,

And some Village,— Though or Maybe?

Simply squishy, suppositious."

All things special and propitious,

Weather wishous or delicious

They pronounced both mad and vicious.

"Bonny burdies and absurdies

Spinning tunes on hurdy-gurdies

We transform to dirty wordies" —

Bonny burdies and absurdies,

Happy tunes on hurdy-gurdies.

Seven

So 'mid rocks and scrubby sages
Shrinking from those winds of whims,
These crazed demons take to shouting
"Silly Belles and Phoney Nims
Do not multiply yours sims,
Here are Information Hymns!
Border ballads of disorder,
Siren songs on Pan's recorder —
Bad words — Silence! — come to order!
Here are Information Hymns,
Hear our Information Hymns."

Eight

Demon dumbsters Don't and Never

Dance a puppet pantomime

Faster masters of disasters

Raining ruin out of time

Growing rich in runic crime

Through this coo-coo clock of rhyme.

All the simplies and the dimplies,

All the smarties and the pimplies,

Look and giggle at your disease

Demon dumbsters caught for ever

In this coo-coo clock of rhyme.

Nine

And the Funny Nims inflected,
(Clearly here the spell they're under)
List the Lady's ludic lisping,
While the Lord of mimic thunder
Shook the Silly Belles asunder,
Turning all that world to wonder

At a Lady sailing hither
Shedding starlight like that river,
Called the noble Twaddlequiver —
Lady Luminosity!
Lady Luminosity!

Ten

Past the Land Transoceanic,

Past the vast Immensett, — See!

Demons turn to Demon Lovers

At the great Invention Tree,

Singing "Beatific Lady,

We have come here to be free."

Then the Bos and Nims and Dongs

Show how synonymphy songs

Sung to homophonic gongs

Can set time to run for ever

In this coo-coo clock of rhyme.

Afterword: The Legend of *The Invention Tree*

Far far away in the Land of Lovely Language is a world ruled by the Lord and Lady Luminosity. In this world All the Fabulous Creatures live happily ever after because of the song of a Vision Bird, who dwelt once upon a time in his secret ancient home. There he sings a neverending song praising the beauty of the Lady Luminosity. So pleasing is the song of the Vision Bird to the Lady and her Lord that their happiness radiates across the world to All the Fabulous Creatures. As All the Fabulous Creatures join in the song of the Vision Bird, the world becomes the Land of Lovely Language.

But in that once upon a time of ages gone by, two of the Fabulous Creatures refused to join the chorus of song. As their world turned outside in, it became Isolation Island, at whose chaotic center suddenly appeared the fearful Impossibilla Tree, where no birds sing.

When that island's Nonsongs dismally drifted down the Land of Lovely Language, the Lady Luminosity began hearing in their birdless songs the unheard melodies of the Impossible Would Land she had always known. Then it was that the Invention Tree appeared in its full glory out of its secret fractal covert, turning all the world to wonder at the neverending magic of the Impossible Would Land. And ever since, in the Land Transoceanic, the world is music everywhere.

When can this glory fade?
O the wild change they made!
All the world wonder'd.
Honour the change they made!
Wordless their light parade,
Noble and number'd!

About the Author and Artist

Jerome McGann teaches at the University of Virginia. His most recent book is the pamphlet from Prickly Paradigm Press, *Are the Humanities Inconsequent?*. "The Invention Tree" is one of a set of prosodic parodies of Edward Lear and Lewis Carroll, *Poems for People of Uncertain Age.*

Susan Bee is a painter, editor, and book artist, living in New York City. Her artist's books include collaborations with Susan Howe, Johanna Drucker, Charles Bernstein, Regis Bonvicino, and Jerome Rothenberg. Bee is coeditor of *M/E/A/N/I/N/G* Online. She will have a solo show at Accola Griefen Gallery in May-June 2013. Her website is at: http://epc.buffalo.edu/authors/bee/

About Chax Press

Chax Press is a 501(c)(3) nonprofit organization, founded in 1984, that has published more than 130 books, including fine art editions and trade editions of literature and book arts works.

For more information, please see our web site at *http://chax.org*

Chax Press is supported by individual contributions, and in part by the Tucson Pima Art Council and the Arizona Commission on the Arts, with funds from the State of Arizona and the National Endowment for the Arts.

TUCSON PIMA ARTS COUNCIL

Arizona Commission on the Arts

NATIONAL ENDOWMENT FOR THE ARTS